THE

Good
Morning
Journal

THE
Good
Morning
Journal

*Powerful Prompts and Reflections
to Start Every Day*

MARC AND ANGEL CHERNOFF

A TARCHERPERIGEE BOOK

tarcherperigee

An imprint of Penguin Random House LLC
penguinrandomhouse.com

Most TarcherPerigee books are available at special quantity discounts for bulk
purchase for sales promotions, premiums, fund-raising, and educational needs.
Special books or book excerpts also can be created to fit specific needs.
For details, write: SpecialMarkets@penguinrandomhouse.com.

ISBN: 9780593541289

Library of Congress Control Number: 2022939811

Printed in the United States of America
2nd Printing

Interior art: Drop pattern © L. Kramer / Shutterstock;
sunburst © Tolchik / Shutterstock

Book design by Kristin del Rosario

To you, for choosing yourself today.
For thinking not just outside the box,
but like there is no box.
And for investing in yourself,
caring for yourself,
and becoming a reliable part
of your own support system.

INTRODUCTION

Too often, people overestimate the significance of one big, defining moment and underestimate the value of making good decisions and tiny steps of progress on a daily basis.

You're probably familiar with what's known as the Serenity Prayer. It goes like this:

> *God, grant me the serenity to accept the things I cannot change, courage to change the things I can, and wisdom to know the difference.*

There's an important lesson here—one that's very often glossed over.

When a chaotic reality is swirling around us, we often try to relieve our anxiety by exerting our will over external things we cannot control.

It helps us stave off one of the most dreaded feelings: complete powerlessness.

With that in mind, we have good news and bad news.

The bad news is that, generally speaking, almost everything is outside your control. What other people do, whether it will rain tomorrow, whether your efforts will be appreciated—all these outcomes depend on factors that aren't *you*.

But that's also the good news.

The friction and frustration created by trying to change things that you cannot change are the crucible where a ton of unhappiness is born. Accepting that most things are outside your influence gives you explicit permission to let them unfold as they may.

Stoic philosopher Epictetus put it this way:

> *Some things are in our control and others not. Things in our control are opinion, pursuit, desire, aversion, and, in a word, whatever are our own actions. Things not in our control are body, property, reputation, command, and, in one word, whatever are not our own actions.*

We need to overcome the three big *"uns"* that so many of us struggle with daily: *un*happy, *un*convinced things will ever change, *un*sure what to do next. And that begins with understanding what you can control and what you cannot.

The mental shift here is not easy. Most of us have spent a lifetime worrying about things that we can't control. Society practically encourages this. For most, it's a bona fide habit—one that should be replaced with a healthy understanding of how much we can actually change. Again, though, it's hard to wrap your mind around all this when you're constantly being told "Why don't you just get over it?" or "Just let it go."

We've all heard some version of this advice before. And it passes the sniff test, to a certain extent.

After all, time heals all wounds, right? Well, yes . . . sort of. Given enough time, most emotional pain will diminish—that's true. But getting over it leaves scars.

In the emotional sense, scars equal baggage—baggage we carry with us into every aspect of our lives. These scars grow and accumulate until one day you wake up suffering from one or more of the three "uns" (*un*happy, *un*convinced things will ever change, *un*sure what to do next).

So don't get over it. Go through it, one step at a time.

Honestly, we understand the desire to get over difficult experiences or situations rather than to face them. Revisiting painful memories or facing our present demons is really, really hard.

However, as most of us have learned the hard way, ignoring a problem doesn't make it go away.

Unresolved issues in your life take up residence in your mind and influence your decisions, your relationships, and your attitudes. They rob you of your happiness and potential, one day at a time.

Of course, doing the hard yet necessary things to resolve your issues and heal your wounds can feel impossible. This is how Angel and I felt a decade ago when we were knocked down and stuck in a rut after simultaneously losing two loved ones—including Angel's dear brother—to suicide and illness. It was nearly impossible to make any progress at all when we didn't feel we had the strength to push forward.

So if you're feeling this way now—that it's impossible to make significant progress today—you aren't wrong for feeling what you feel. In many cases, you're right: significant progress comes gradually with time and consistency. It's all about taking one tiny positive step at a time and staying the course. Truly, it's about the power of tiny changes.

Think about the fact that it takes only a one-degree change in temperature to convert water to vapor or ice to water. It's such a tiny change—just one step in a different direction—and yet the results are dramatic. A tiny change can make all the difference in the world.

Now consider another example where a tiny change is compounded by time and distance. Perhaps you're trying to travel somewhere specific, yet you're off course by just one degree in the wrong direction . . .

After a mile, you would be off course by over ninety feet.

If you were trying to travel from San Francisco to Washington, DC, you would land near Baltimore, Maryland, over forty miles away from your desired destination.

Traveling around the world from Washington, DC, back to Washington, DC, you'd miss by 435 miles and end up near Boston instead.

In a spaceship traveling to the moon, a one-degree error would have you missing the moon by over 4,100 miles.

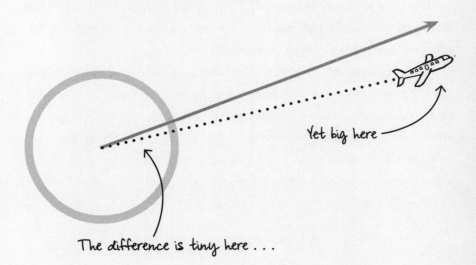

Yet big here —

The difference is tiny here . . .

You get the idea—over time and distance, a mere one-degree change in course makes a significant difference. This same philosophy holds true in various aspects of our lives too. The tiniest things we do each day—positive and negative alike—can make all the difference. They bring us either closer to or farther away from where we ultimately want to be. And yet we mostly ignore this reality. We default to behaving as if our daily actions won't ever be significant. Or, again, we try to exert control over the bigger things we have no control over.

Think about it . . .

How many people uphold unhealthy and unproductive habits?

How many people procrastinate on the next positive step?

How many people live every day of their lives moving one degree away from where they ultimately want to be?

The key thing now is to not be one of them.

Truth be told, everyone travels twenty-four hours a day, whether they're moving in the right direction or not.

How much richer would your life be if you committed yourself to making just one degree of effort to improve something about your situation each day?

And even though it will surely be harder than doing nothing, it doesn't even have to be anything that difficult. You just need to muster up the courage to break free from the status quo and take one tiny step forward today, and then do it again tomorrow.

That's precisely what *The Good Morning Journal* is all about—taking a tiny step forward every day, first thing in morning.

The Good Morning Journal Practice

Don't just think outside the box when you awake to a new day.

Think like there is no box!

Ease your worried mind by tuning out the excess noise in your head for a few minutes each morning.

You know how you turn down the volume on the stereo or your headphones when you need a moment to think clearly? The same is true for life in general. The noise you need to cut out first? That's the mental noise we hear all too often—the busy, worried thoughts screaming over our sanity.

Turning down the stereo or headphones refocuses your mind and offers you peace and clarity when you need it most. You don't really think about how or why this makes such a huge difference, but you just know that it does.

Now it's time to apply this same strategy to all the other noise in your life, starting with the noise in your head. And although that's not quite as easy to do as turning down the music on your devices, the good news is you can quiet your mind and train it to think more peacefully and rationally simply by reminding yourself to do so every day.

The best tool for the job? You guessed it: morning journaling. It's a simple practice of self-reflection that keeps you on track by putting peaceful, productive thoughts at the top of your mind, even when life gets noisy. In many little ways, it provides the one-degree shift your mind needs on a daily basis.

Remind yourself that the mind is like a muscle, and just like every muscle in the human body, it needs to be exercised to gain strength. It needs to be trained daily to grow and develop gradually over time. If you haven't pushed your mind in thousands of little positive ways over time, of course it will struggle when things get overwhelmingly stressful. Daily self-reflection is one of the simplest and most powerful tools for doing this. A mind well trained by consistent daily self-reflection has the right thoughts and perspectives queued up and ready for retrieval at a moment's notice.

Last year Angel wrote a short email newsletter about one of our first students, who had graduated with a PhD a few years earlier from one of the most prestigious universities in the United States and who is now an executive for one of the world's fastest-growing tech companies. She continues to be our go-to example of why daily self-reflection is so powerful.

Throughout grade school and high school, she desperately wrestled with a form of dyslexia that made reading and writing a monumental challenge. She spent kindergarten through twelfth grade in language-based special needs classes. And during a parent-teacher conference when she was in tenth grade, one of her teachers informed her parents that it was extremely unlikely she would ever receive a high school diploma.

So how did she do it? How did she push herself to rise up and overcome the odds? "Daily self-reflection through journaling," she confirmed to us when we interviewed her last year for a recent side project. "The daily journaling and self-reflection ritual you guys set me up with, and held me accountable to, changed everything! While it may sound cliché to some people, it's absolutely not—journaling is a powerful tool! I literally gave myself the perspective I needed to see that the naysayers were wrong about me. I learned to see and feel what I needed to see and feel, every single day, to gradually move my life forward."

Journaling truly is a priceless tool for self-reflection and making real progress in life.

Oprah keeps a journal. Eminem keeps a journal. Lady Gaga keeps a journal.

Successful people all over the world—those who consistently make positive changes and progress in their lives—reflect daily in a journal.

Because if you want to get somewhere in life, you need a map, and a journal is that map.

How to Use This Journal

The journal prompts that follow are ones we have personally used over the past fifteen years to nudge ourselves, and hundreds of coaching clients, into self-reflection. They will make you aware of your subconscious beliefs and assumptions. And they will help you think through situations, big and small, to make better decisions.

Also note that since two of us—Marc and Angel—authored this work together, you may notice the voice change from one section of the work to the next without us specifying exactly whose voice it is. This is done purposefully to keep the focus on you, the reader. The goal is to leverage the prompts and supporting anecdotes as a gateway to deep and personal self-reflection.

You'll find 365 prompts in total. We recommend answering one each morning, but if you prefer to tackle a few at a time, that's great too. Set a fifteen-minute timer, tune out distractions, and write without self-censoring. Remember, it takes roughly sixty-six days to form a new habit. So at the very least, for the next nine weeks (and maybe longer if it feels right), wake up every morning and use these daily questions to look at the right side of your life, and you will rewire your brain and change your life.

Let's begin.

What's something true about yourself that you need to embrace more openly and lovingly today?

What's something small that always brings you peace when you think about it? Why?

Write down five things on your bucket list and why they are important.

How do you spend the majority of your free time right now?

With the resources you have right now, what can you do a little bit of every day to bring yourself closer to where you ultimately want to be?

What did you want to be when you grew up? Why do you think that mattered to you when you were younger?

How will today matter one year from now?

What's something you often take too personally even though, logically, you know better? How would removing this burden from your mind feel in this moment?

What has your inner voice been trying to tell you lately?

What distractions have been getting the best of you lately? How can you gradually refocus your energy?

You matter. Practice loving yourself instead of simply loving the idea of other people loving you. Practice respecting yourself, caring for yourself, and becoming a reliable part of your own support system. No more waiting on others to choose you. Choose yourself, starting now.

What's one (true) reason you're good enough and ready enough right now?

Who would you be, and what else would you see about your present life situation, if you removed the thought that's been worrying you?

What's one thing you could be incredibly grateful for right now if you truly wanted to be grateful?

Where do you spend most of your time, and where would you like to spend more time? Why?

How have you helped someone recently? Who?
When?

Whose life have you had the greatest impact on over
the past five years? How?

What's the best part of being you, right here, right now?

What is your greatest skill or talent? How does it help you and others?

How have you been making consistent progress in your life recently?

What's the next small yet important step you need to take?

When life feels like an emotional roller coaster, as it does for so many of us right now, just do your best to steady yourself with simple rituals. Make the bed. Water the plants. Rinse off your own bowl and spoon. Simplicity attracts calmness, peace, and wisdom.

Is it possible to know the truth without challenging it first? Why or why not?

How do you personally define success in life?

If we learn from our mistakes, why are we always so afraid to make a mistake?

How old would you be if you didn't know how old you are today? Why?

What's something you do differently than most people? Why?

In the haste of your daily life, what are you not seeing?

Is it more important to do what you love or to love what you are doing? What's the difference?

What is your number one goal for the next six months? Why?

Are you generally happy with yourself right now?
Why or why not?

What makes you proud?

Trust the Journey

It may not seem like it right now, but better days are coming. The test always comes before the merit. The struggle always precedes the strength. You have to endure breakdowns to find breakthroughs. Take it one day at a time and trust the journey. It will make sense, in time.

Of course, it takes a while to get comfortable with it all.

I was lucky enough to have a very wise grandmother who coached me through my overwhelming feelings of hopelessness when I was just a teenager. And I was smart enough to write a journal entry about the conversation I had with her, so I could remember her wisdom decades later. Let me give you a little taste of that conversation:

I sat there in her living room staring at her through teary eyes. "I feel lost and alone and completely out of my mind," I said. "I don't know what's wrong with me."

"Why do you feel that way?" she delicately asked.

"Because I'm neurotic and self-conscious and regretful, and so much more all at once," I said.

"And you don't think everyone feels the way you do sometimes?" she asked.

"Not like this!" I proclaimed.

"Well, honey, you're wrong," she said. "If you think you know someone who never feels the way you do right now—who never feels a bit lost and alone, and downright confused and crazy—you just don't know enough about them. Every one of us contains a measure of 'crazy' that moves us in strange, often perplexing ways. This side of us is necessary; it's part of our human ability to think, adapt, and grow. It's part of being intelligent," she said. "No great mind has ever existed without a touch of this kind of madness."

I sat silently for a moment. My eyes gazed from her eyes to the ground and back to her eyes again. "So you're saying I should want to feel like this?"

"To an extent," she said. "Let me put it this way: taking all your feelings seriously all the time and letting them drive you into misery is a waste of your incredible spirit. You alone get to choose what matters and what doesn't. The meaning of everything in your life is the meaning you give it . . ."

"I guess," I replied under my breath.

She continued, "And sometimes how you feel simply won't align with how you want to feel—it's mostly just your subconscious mind's way of helping you look at things from a different perspective. These feelings will come and go quickly as long as you let them go . . . as long as you consciously acknowledge them and then push through them. At least, that's what I've learned to do for myself, out of necessity, on a very regular basis. So you and I are actually struggling through this one together, honey. And I'm also pretty certain we're not the only ones."

We shared another moment of silence, then my lips curled up slightly, and I cracked a smile. "Thank you, Grandma," I said.

When have you worked hard and loved every minute of it?

What are you looking forward to in the next forty-eight hours? Why?

Who is the strongest person you know? What is their strength?

What are your top three priorities in life right now?

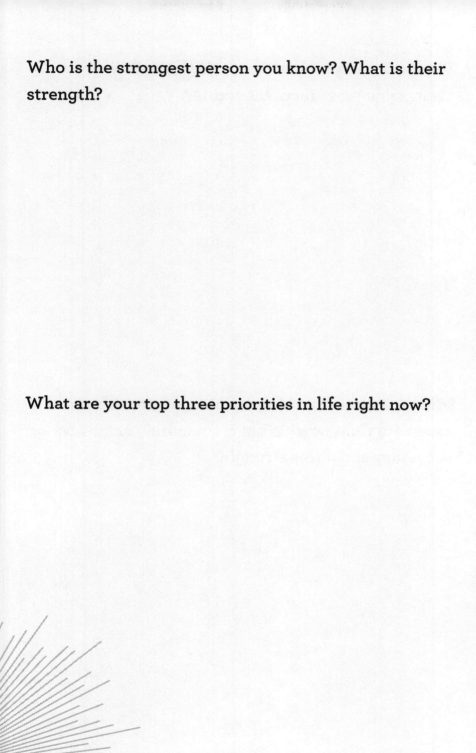

What worries you most about the future? What excites you most about the future?

What's the hardest thing you're trying to achieve or cope with right now? What is something small and necessary about this struggle?

What's one unchangeable reality you're still subconsciously resisting? What can you do right now to ease your mind into the acceptance of this reality?

How has your daily environment been affecting you recently?

How can you give yourself a little extra time and space to make the right decisions on a daily basis?

What are you holding on to that's holding you down? And what can you let go of right now (without losing a thing)?

The ability to not overreact or engage too deeply in life's drama keeps your mind clear, your heart at peace, and you fully composed in otherwise uncontrollable situations. Yes, with practice, calmness can be your superpower.

If you had to choose or make one for yourself, what would be your life motto?

What's something you have that everyone wants?

What do you need most right now?

What does the child inside you still long for?

What is one thing that you are totally sure of in this moment?

What never fails to frustrate you and also teach you?

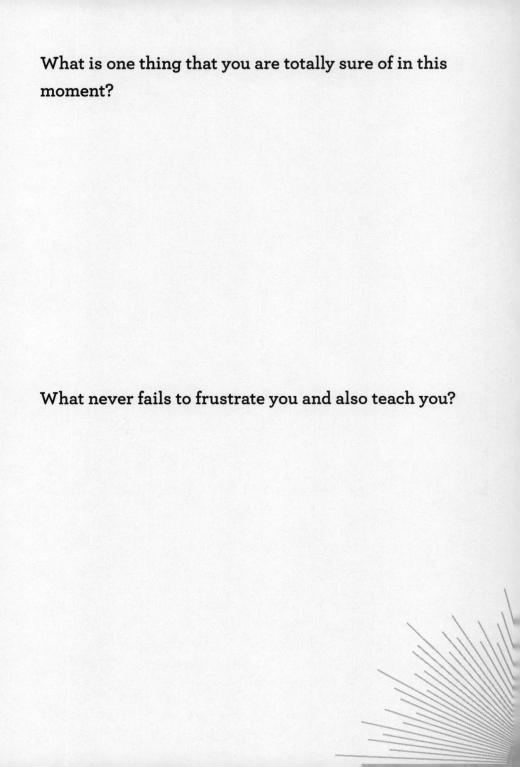

What's a common misconception people have about you?

What's something that's harder for you than it is for most people? How is this also a slight benefit?

How far have you come? How much have you grown?
Think about the specifics of your recent and long-
term growth. What have you not given yourself
enough credit for?

What can someone do to grab your attention?

The secret to being grateful is no secret. You choose to be grateful a little bit every day. So just do your best to find gratitude for what you have today. Because some of it is a blessing. And nothing lasts forever.

What do you usually think about on long drives (or flights) home?

What simple fact do you wish more people understood?

If you could do it all over again, would you change anything about the past twenty-four hours?

How would you describe your present in three words? And how would you like to describe your future in three words?

When was the last time you felt lucky?

How do you deal with loneliness? Who or what helps you feel more alive and whole?

What do you know well enough to teach to others?
What value could this add to their lives?

What's a quick decision you once made that changed
your life? How did it change things?

What have you lost interest in recently? Why?

What activity makes your life easier after you do it?

Choose Differently

Our challenge to you, starting today, is this:

Live your life not as a bystander . . .

not as a prisoner to the false beliefs and stories that keep you stuck in your seat.

Live in this world, on this day and every day hereafter, as an active participant. Every morning, ask yourself what is real and important to you, and then find the courage, wisdom, and willpower to build your day around your answer.

It's your choice.

Your choice!

You are choosing right now.

And if you're choosing . . .

to complain . . .

to blame . . .

to be stuck in the past . . .

to act like a victim . . .

to feel insecure . . .

to feel anger . . .

to feel hate . . .

to be naive . . .

to ignore your intuition . . .

to ignore good advice . . .

to give up . . .

then it's time to choose differently!

But let us also remind you that you are not alone. Generations of human beings in your family tree have chosen. Human beings around the world have chosen. We all have chosen at one time or another. And we stand behind you now, whispering:

Choose to be present.

Choose to be positive.

Choose to forgive yourself.

Choose to forgive others.

Choose to see your value.

Choose to see the possibilities.

Choose to find meaning.

Choose to prove you're not a helpless victim.

Choose to let go of your false beliefs and stories.

Choose to find strength in the truth—*your truth*—so that you can take real steps forward, starting today.

How can you let calmness be your superpower today?

What's something small that's worth working on today, regardless of what other people think? Why is it important to you?

When did you not speak up when you feel that you should have? What do you still need to say and resolve in your heart?

What is your favorite quote? What does it mean to you?

Where or who do you turn to when you need good advice? What was the last good piece of advice you received?

What artistic medium do you use to express yourself? What do you enjoy about it?

How many hours of television (or general passive screen time) do you average in a week? A month? A year?

Why are you ready to level up right now? Why are the painful parts of this process totally worth it?

What does "a new beginning" mean to you right now?

What are you scared of right now? Why? Is it truly fear, or is it uncertainty?

Progress and inner peace both begin the moment you take a deep breath and choose not to allow another person or event to control your thoughts. You are not what happened. You are what you choose to become in this moment. Let go, breathe, and begin again.

What is something you've always wanted but don't have yet? What pieces do you have?

What's something you said you'd never do but have since done? Why? What did you learn?

When you look deep into the past, what do you miss the most?

What's something from the past that you don't miss at all?

What recently reminded you of how fast time flies?

What's the most valuable thing you own? How does it benefit your life?

What's something about the present moment that makes it the perfect time to begin (again)?

What's one privilege you have that you often take for granted?

What's something that used to drive you crazy but that no longer bothers you? Why?

What is truly worth focusing on today? What is *not*?

When certain people and
opportunities close their doors
on you, take it as an indication
that they do not have a role
in your next chapter.
It's not rejection, it's evolution.
It's progress.

What is something you don't understand but
sometimes pretend you do?

What is the biggest obstacle that stands in your way
right now?

Who depends on you? What do they depend on
you for?

Who has had the greatest impact on your life over the
past ten years? What have you learned from them?

Are you happy with where you stand with your priorities today? What needs more attention, or less?

In one year from today, how do you think your life will be different?

How would you spend your ideal day if you could have it exactly your way?

What do you often think about when you lie awake in bed?

What's something most people don't know about your future hopes and dreams?

When you have a random hour of free time, what do you usually do?

What do you worry about the most when you think of your goals?

Do you need to forgive yourself for anything? What and why?

Carry You Forward

The seemingly useless happenings add up to something. The minimum-wage job you had when you were just starting out. The evenings you spent socializing with colleagues you never see anymore. The hours you spent writing thoughts on a personal blog that no one reads. The contemplations about elaborate future plans that never came to be. All those lonely nights spent reading novels and news columns and comic strips and fashion magazines and questioning your own principles on life and sex and religion and whether you're good enough just the way you are. All of this has strengthened you. All of this has led you to every success you've ever had. All of this has made you who you are today.

I can tell you from my own life experience that I've found love, lost it, found it, lost it, and then found it once again. But each time, what I found was more incredible than the last. So remember that everyone suffers at some point in life. You are not alone. Everyone feels lost at times. The key is using your experiences to grow. When you apply what you're learning to your future choices and actions, you move forward, not backward. You become stronger and wiser. It's not easy, but it's worth it in the end.

And yes, I know you have gone through numerous ups and downs that have made you who you are today. Over the years, so many things have happened—things that have changed your perspective, taught you lessons, and forced your spirit to grow. As time passes, nobody stays the same, but some people will still tell you that you have changed. Respond to them by saying, "Of course I've changed. That's what life is all about. I'm still the same human being, just a little stronger and wiser now than I ever was before."

The bottom line is that you are a product of your past, but you don't have to be a prisoner of it. It may be hard, but you can *let go*! You *can* accept the feeling of not knowing exactly where you're going next and train yourself to love and appreciate this freedom. Because it is only when you are suspended in the air, with no destination in sight, that you force your wings to open fully so you can fly. And as you soar around, you still may not know where you're traveling to. But that's not what's important. What's important is the opening of your wings. You may not know where you're headed, but you know that as long as your wings are spread, the winds will carry you forward.

What's one step forward you've been thinking about taking for far too long?

What is the best advice you ever received?

What positive changes have you made in your life recently?

What do you admire most about your parents or caregivers?

If you could go back in time and change things, what would you change about the week that just passed?

Who would you like to forgive? Forgive for what?

At what point during the past five years have you felt lost and alone? What have you learned since then?

What do you want more of in your life right now? What's the simplest way to get a little more of it?

What do you want less of in your life? Why?

What's something new you recently learned about yourself?

Life humbles us as we age. We gradually realize how much nonsense we've wasted time on. And we gradually realize how precious the present truly is. Let this sink in today. The afternoon always understands what the morning never even suspected.

What has been the most defining moment in your life during this past year?

What's something you've moved on from that once meant the world to you? What's something you love today that you never even knew you needed in your life?

What are two things life has taught you recently?

What is the one thing you would most like to change about the world?

Where do you find inspiration on an average day?

In three sentences, who are you in this moment?

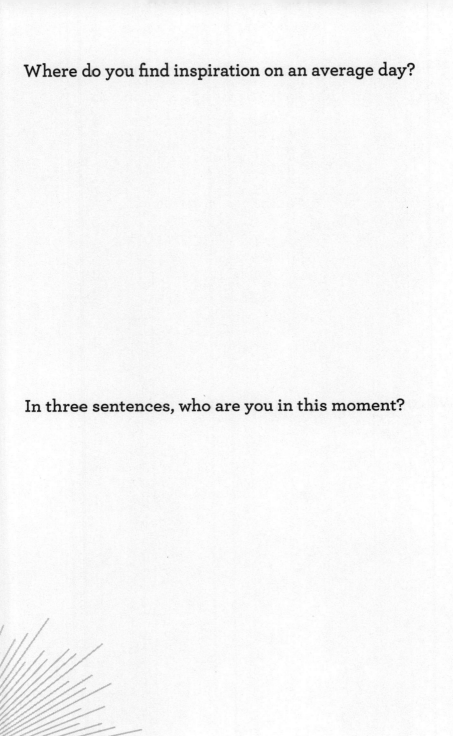

If life is so short, why do we do so many things we don't like and like so many things we don't do?

What lifts your spirits when life gets you down?

What's something your parents or caregivers never taught you that you intend to instill in others?

What idea gets you most excited about the future?

I will be too busy working
on my own grass to notice
if yours is greener.
I will speak like I love myself.
Move like I love myself.
Eat like I love myself.
And live like I love myself.
Today!

What important life lesson did you learn the hard way?

Do you ask enough questions, or do you settle for what you know? Explain.

Who do you sometimes compare yourself with? Why?

What would you do differently if you knew nobody would judge you?

Do you celebrate the things you do have? If so, how? If not, what deserves a moment of celebration right now?

What is the difference between living and existing?

Which is worse, failing or never trying? Why?

If not now, then when? What specifically comes to mind when you read that question?

What are you holding on to that you need to let go of?

When you are eighty-five years old, what will matter to you the most?

More of What You Really Need

Eventually, most of us end up settling in some parts of our lives. We let go of certain ideals and dreams, we compromise, and we make trade-offs. We gradually learn that we can't have everything we want, because not every outcome in life can be perfectly controlled. But if we pay close attention, we also learn that we can make the best of every outcome and still get a lot of what we want in life if we manage our time, energy, and attitudes effectively.

And these realizations collectively lead to an interesting question:

When should you settle or compromise, and when should you continue fighting hard for what you ideally want to achieve?

There is no one-size-fits-all answer to this question, but when you encounter a situation that forces you to choose between compromising and fighting forward against the opposition, it might help to also ask yourself:

"Do I really need this, or do I just kinda want it?"

Being able to distinguish needs from wants is essential in every walk of life. Never let go of an outcome you truly need in your life, but be reasonably flexible on the outcomes you want but could live just fine without.

In other words, choose your battles wisely and don't let "perfect" become the enemy of "great." Remind yourself that what you pay attention to grows. So focus on what really matters and let go of what does not.

Don't give up 50 percent of your life to working fifty-hour weeks at a job that makes you absolutely miserable. Don't abandon your sanity for the wrong reasons. Don't neglect lifelong goals and dreams that have withstood the test of time and that still bring incredible meaning into your life.

If you really need something, fight hard for it!

But for everything else, let go a little. Loosen your grip, compromise . . . settle.

Settle on less of the unessential to get more of what you really need and want in life.

Who do you love most and how will you act on that love today?

What's a belief you hold that many people disagree with?

What can you do today that you weren't capable of a year ago?

What's something small that's been stressing you out recently? What can you do to improve your response today?

What do you love about your present life situation, despite the challenges that exist? Who do you love today, despite the quirks they have?

Have you done anything recently that you will likely remember for the rest of your life?

What's something you could invest in today that would absolutely yield a positive return five years from now?

If you had a friend who spoke to you in the same way that you sometimes speak to yourself, how long would you allow this person to be your friend? Explain.

What activities make you lose track of time? List five.

If you had to teach something for eight hours to a small group of people, what would you teach and why?

You can't do it all. Be mindful today. Say no to good things so that you are able to say yes to important things. Truly, the quality of your life just a few short years from now will greatly depend on how well you respect your personal priorities.

When is it time to stop calculating risks and rewards and to just do what you know is right? How have you lived true to this philosophy recently?

What life experience makes you smile inside just thinking about it?

When it's all said and done, will you have said more than you've done? What needs more doing today?

What life lesson did you have to experience firsthand before you fully understood it?

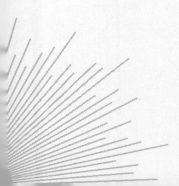

What simple gesture have you recently witnessed that renewed your hope in humanity?

What is the number one quality that makes someone a good leader?

What's one bad habit you want to break? What's one positive habit you can replace it with?

What is your favorite place on earth? Why?

What do you love to practice, even when it gets hard?

What questions do you often ask yourself? List three.

The majority of what's stressing you out today probably won't matter a month from now. Shake it off, reset, and bring your attention back to what's important. Remember, what you focus on grows. Stop micromanaging your time and start better managing your focus so that you can move forward.

What's been bothering you the most lately?

What's the most difficult decision you've ever made in your life? Why was it so difficult?

What is worth the pain every single day?

In order of importance, how would you rank these: happiness, money, community, health, family, fame, peace, and validation?

What do your most recent actions say about your priorities? What kind of silent progress would you like to make in your life in the next month?

What's one distraction that has been getting the best of you lately? Why?

What truly matters to you most right now? How much time each day are you investing in it?

What has the fear of failure stopped you from doing in the past year?

Who would you like to please the most on a daily basis? Why?

Which one of your responsibilities do you wish you could get rid of? What would you like to replace it with?

When do you usually feel most content and at peace?

What have you done in the past year that feels like progress?

Best to Be Mindful

Goals are important. All journeys of change must begin with a goal. And you also must have determination in order to achieve your goals. However, what do you think happens when you are too determined or too obsessed with a goal? You begin to nurture another belief: who you are right now is not good enough.

Years ago, I became overly obsessive in my efforts to meditate. As my interest in meditation grew, I began to increasingly say to myself, "I am not good enough," and "I have to be better at this." I began to notice various imperfections within myself that needed to be "fixed."

My over-the-top efforts to meditate for extensive periods of time opened the door to lots of self-criticism and stress. Thankfully, however, I realized that my obsession with meditation had made me forget one of the basic objectives of the practice—self-acceptance.

So the bottom line is this: you have to accept yourself as you are and then commit to personal growth. If you think you are absolutely perfect already, you will not make any positive efforts to grow. But constantly criticizing yourself is just as counterproductive as doing nothing, because you will never be able to build new positive changes into your life when you're obsessively focused on your flaws.

The key is to remind yourself that you are already good enough; you just need more practice. Change your mantra from "I have to be better" to "I will do my absolute best today." The second mantra is far more effective because it actually prompts you to take positive action every day while simultaneously accepting the reality that every effort may not be perfect.

Or, to put it another way, do your best to be mindful.

Mindfulness as a daily ritual is the ultimate challenge and practice. It's a way of living, of being, of seeing, of tapping into the full power of your humanity.

Ready to get started?

It's simple but far from easy. Practice...

- **Being aware of what's happening in the present moment without wishing it were different**

- **Enjoying each pleasant experience without holding on when it changes (which it will)**

- **Being with each unpleasant experience without fearing it will always be this way (which it won't)**

Ritualize this kind of mindfulness into your daily routines, and you will undoubtedly change the way you spend the rest of your life.

What is necessary and true about where you are right now? How does it feel to embrace this present reality?

In what way do you sometimes turn to others for the validation you can always give to yourself? How will you choose yourself today?

What is the nicest thing someone has ever done for you?

What do you see when you look one year into the future?

What are the primary components of a happy life?

What's your favorite true story that you enjoy sharing with others?

Right now, at this moment, what do you want most?

What are you waiting for? Be honest with yourself.
What are you still waiting around for in your life?
What are you delaying?

What makes love last a lifetime?

What unexpected good has come to you from past struggles?

Eventually you will end up where you need to be, doing the right things, alongside the right people. Patience is the key. And remember, patience is not about waiting, it is the ability to maintain a positive outlook while working hard for what you believe in.

What's the most important lesson you've learned in the past year?

Based on your current daily actions and routines, where would you expect to be one year from today?

What was your last major accomplishment? How long did it take, really, to accomplish?

Through all of life's twists and turns, who has been there for you?

What or who has been distracting you from what matters most?

What are you looking forward to in the next week and month?

What are you uncertain about right now? What could bring more clarity?

What makes you weird?

What small lesson did life teach you or remind you of yesterday?

Who makes you feel good about yourself on a regular basis?

Too often we take for granted and "wait away" the vast majority of our lives. Truly, some people wait all day for 5 p.m., all week for Friday, all year for the holidays, all their lives for happiness. Don't be one of them.

What do you like most about your career/work? What do you dislike most about your career/work?

What's something you don't like to do that you are still really good at?

What makes you feel secure and confident? Explain.

What is your favorite sound? Why?

What is the number one motivator in your life right now?

What are some of the best compliments you've received in your life?

How many friends do you have that you talk to regularly? What do you typically talk about?

How much money per month is enough for you to live comfortably? What does "living comfortably" entail, in your opinion?

What was the last thing you furiously argued about with someone? Was progress made?

What's one small risk you believe is worth taking in the months ahead? What's the first step? What's required afterward to make the risk worth it?

Life Is Making Room

You can't lose what you never had, you can't keep what's not yours, and you can't hold on to something that does not want to stay. But you can drive yourself mad by trying. What you need to realize is that most things are a part of your life only because you keep thinking about them. Stop holding on to what hurts and make room for what feels right! Do not let what is out of your control interfere with all the things you can control. In other words, say goodbye to what didn't work out so that you can say hello to what might right now.

In life, goodbyes are a gift. When certain people walk away from you or certain opportunities close their doors on you, there is no need to hold on to them or pray to keep them present in your life. If they close you out, take it as a direct indication that these people, circumstances, and opportunities are not part of the next chapter in your life. It's a hint that your personal growth requires someone different or something more, and life is making room.

Realize that life is simply a collection of little chances for happiness, each lived one moment at a time. That some time each day should be spent noticing the beauty in the space between the big events. That moments of dreaming and sunsets and refreshing breezes cannot be bettered. But most of all, realize that life is about being present, watching and listening and working without a clock and without anticipation of results at every moment, and sometimes, on really good days, about letting these little moments fill your heart with intense gratitude.

Truth be told, you will inevitably, whether tomorrow or on your deathbed, come to wish that you had spent less time worrying and rushing through your life, and more time actually being mindful and appreciative of each present day.

The bottom line is that mindset is everything. Despite the real-world challenges and stress you face, the biggest and most complex obstacle you have to personally overcome on a daily basis is your own mind. Yes, almost everything you think and do is a reflection of what you believe about yourself and your life situation. Thus, it's not what you broadcast to everyone else that determines the trajectory of your life; it's what you whisper to yourself behind closed doors that has the greatest power and influence.

What's one small example of how you have "customized" your life for the better?

What's something big you've accomplished in the past that once seemed impossible?

If you had the chance to go back in time and change one thing, would you do it? Why or why not? What ripple effects might it have throughout your life?

If the average human life span were sixty years (instead of eighty), how would you live your life differently today?

What do we all have in common?

Do you ever celebrate the green lights when driving?
What metaphorical "green lights" in your life deserve
a moment of recognition right now?

What personal prisons have you built out of fear? If you had only six months left to live, what would you no longer be scared of?

What one thing have you not done that you really want to do before you die?

Since you haven't achieved it yet, what do you have to lose by going for it? What comes to mind when you first read that question?

What small act of kindness were you once shown that you will never forget?

The goal right now is to gradually change your response to what you can't control. To grow stronger on the inside so that almost nothing on the outside can affect your inner peace and wellness without your conscious permission.

What is your happiest childhood memory? What makes it so special?

When do you feel most like yourself? What's the setting and activity?

What's one little thing that makes you undeniably worthy in your own mind right now?

What's something from your past that you are thankful you gave up on? Why?

When was the last time you listened to the sound of your own breathing? Do it again right now. What do you feel in this moment?

What gives your life meaning?

What do you love most about who you are today?

How would you describe the idea of "true freedom" in your own words?

What do you owe yourself a little more of?

What is your greatest strength and your greatest weakness? How are they related?

Most of the time, you can't calm the storm. What you can do is calm yourself, and the storm will eventually pass. Truly, the most powerful and practical changes happen when you decide to take control of what you do have power over instead of craving control over what you don't.

In twenty years, what do you want to remember about the current season of your life?

What are you most excited about in your life right now, today?

What experience from this past year do you appreciate the most?

What is the most enjoyable thing your family has done together in the past three years?

What's the number one change you want to make in your life in the next twelve months?

What are the top three qualities you look for in a friend?

What is your favorite smell? Why?

What recent memory gives you feel-good vibes just thinking about it?

What music do you listen to that lifts your spirits when you're feeling down? Name two songs (and play them if you have a moment).

What would you regret not fully doing, being, or having in your life ten years from today?

A Second Chance at Life

Sometimes you simply have to let go and accept the feeling of not knowing exactly where you're going next and do your best to appreciate this freedom. Truly, endless worrying is a misuse of your incredible creative energy. So do your best to focus mindfully on what's in front of you today. Remind yourself that the most powerful weapon against worry and stress is a healthy mind's ability to choose one present focal point over another.

Are you ready to make a mindset shift? Let me share a quick life-changing story with you that may help you do just that. (Please note that this is a story about suicidal thinking.)

"Today, on my forty-seventh birthday, I reread the suicide note I wrote on my twenty-seventh birthday about two minutes before my girlfriend, Carol, showed up at my apartment and told me, 'I'm pregnant.' Her words were honestly the only reason I didn't follow through with it. Suddenly I felt I had something to live for, and I started making positive changes. It's been a journey, but Carol is now my wife and we've been happily married for nineteen years. And my daughter, who is now a nineteen-year-old university student pursuing a degree in medicine, has two younger brothers.

I reread my suicide note every year on the morning of my birthday as a reminder to be grateful—I am grateful I got a second chance at life."

That's the opening paragraph of an email Marc and I received this past year from an attendee at our annual "Think Better, Live Better" event. Kevin's words continue to remind me that sometimes you have to die a little on the inside first in order to let go and rise again—with your wings fully spread—as a stronger, happier version of yourself.

Marc and I have personally dealt with our fair share of adversity too—losing siblings and best friends to suicide, major health issues, financial and business turmoil, etc.—and we've written a lot about it over the years. But right now, let me just remind you that while you may not be responsible for everything that happened to you in the past, or everything that's happening to you today, you do need to be responsible for undoing the thinking and behavioral patterns these circumstances create.

It's about consciously thinking better so that you can ultimately spread your wings and live better.

The key is to understand that no matter what happens, you can choose your response, which dictates pretty much everything that happens next. Truly, the greatest weapon you have against anxiety, negativity, and stress is your ability to pause, breathe, and choose one present response over another—to train your mind to make the best of what you've got in front of you, even when it's different from what you expected.

How have your expectations of others gotten the best of you recently? How will you remind yourself to ease your expectations today and in the days ahead?

Can there be happiness without sadness? Pleasure without pain? Peace without war? Why or why not? Explain.

What's the number one thing you would like others to remember about you at the end of your life?

What's the closest thing to perfect in your life right now? Why is it "perfect" for you?

What forms of clutter have been complicating your life and diverting you from making meaningful progress? How can you simplify and clear a little bit of space for yourself today?

What past mistakes do you still think about often? What have such errors in judgment taught you?

How does giving yourself full permission to be imperfectly human feel right now? How can you remind yourself to do this more often?

When did you first realize that life is short? How has that experience changed your thinking?

What is the most insensitive thing a person can do?
What is the most gracious thing a person can do?

What is the most spontaneous thing you have ever
done? What sparked the spontaneity?

Do your best to use
disappointment and frustration
to motivate you rather than
to distract you today.
Be mindful. You are in control
of the way you respond to life.

Who and what do you think stand between you and more happiness right now? What options do you have to lower these barriers today, even if it's just by a little bit?

To what degree have you actually controlled the course your life has taken? What's one positive outcome you did control, and what's one you didn't?

What is your earliest childhood memory? What is the
significance of that memory?

What is the best part of growing older?

When you look back over the past month, what single moment stands out?

What motivates you to be your best? Why?

What's one thing you wish you had done differently in the past year? Why? What are the tiny benefits or lessons gained from how it was done?

What will you never give up on?

What do you wish you had spent more time doing five years ago? In five years, what might you wish you had done more of today?

What is the most desirable trait another person can possess? Why?

Do your thing today with as much kindness, humility, and honesty as possible. Do what you do, not for repayment or applause, but because it's what's right. Yep, forget about compensation and popularity. Just focus on goodness and sincerity today. Be the change you want to see!

What are you most grateful for at this moment?

What do you want most out of the average day?

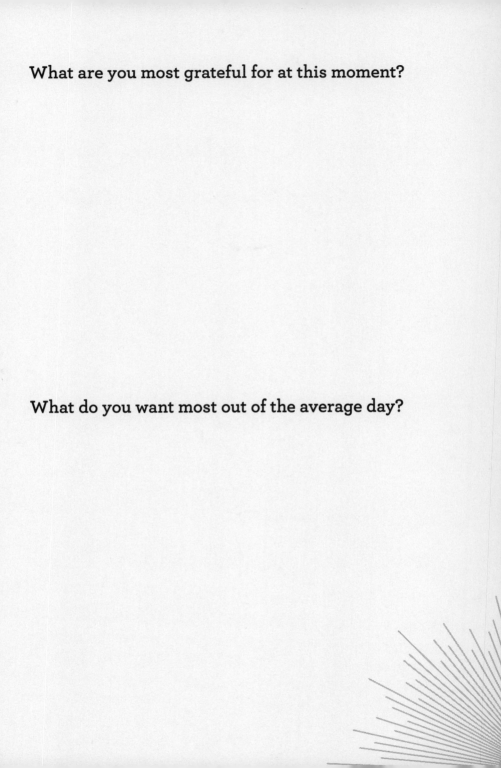

What do you have that you cannot live without?

When you close your eyes, what do you see right now?
Describe it in detail.

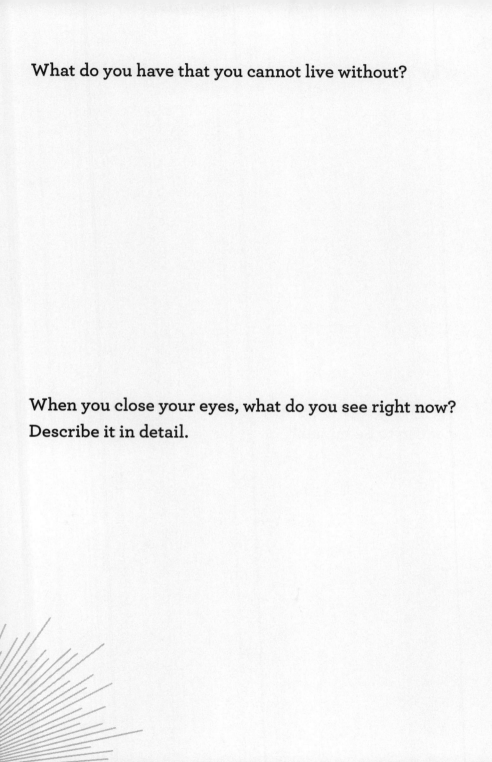

Why must you love someone enough to let them go?

Off the top of your head, in three sentences, what does it mean to be human?

Where would you most like to travel to and why?

If you could live one day of your life over again, what day would you choose?

Why do you matter?

How have you changed in the past five years? What have you learned about yourself?

Restore the Faith

Are you willing to spend a little time every day (as most people aren't) so that you can spend the better part of your life like most people can't?

Think about that question for a moment. Let it sink in. Who you ultimately become is related to what you repeatedly do in life.

And isn't it funny how from one day to the next, nothing seems to change, but when you look back, everything is different? That's the power of daily rituals.

Now it's time to think about your rituals—the little things you do every day that occupy your attention and energy.

Because in many ways, these little things define *you*.

Many of the most significant results you achieve in life—the accolades, the relationships, the love, the lessons—come from these little things.

Regardless of your unique talents, knowledge, and life circumstances, or how you personally define success, you don't suddenly become successful. You become successful—you become an expert—over time based on your rituals.

So, what do your daily rituals look like?

You really have to sort this out and get consistent with what's right for you. Because failure occurs in the same way. All your little daily failures (those that you don't learn and grow from) come together and cause you to fail.

Think in terms of running a business. If you keep failing to do the little things that need to be done (checking the books, making the calls, listening to your customers), you'll wake up one day to find that your business has failed.

It was all the little things you did or didn't do on a daily basis—your rituals—not just one inexplicable, catastrophic event.

Again, think about how this relates to your life. Your life is your "business"!

Your daily rituals literally make or break you, gradually.

And as you build up strong daily rituals to reach your goals, you'll gain something else too: trust in yourself. Each promise kept, each step taken, renews your belief that you can change your life for the better. And it's undoubtedly one of the most important, life-changing things you can do for yourself.

What's one old pattern of behavior that sometimes still sneaks up on you? What's a better alternative today and why?

What kind of old drama or baggage do you still sometimes get caught up in?

Who are you in this moment, without the baggage?

What do you do to relieve stress and reenergize
yourself? How often do you do this?

What do you deliberately do to impress others?

Who do you think of first when you think of the word "successful"? Why?

What's one "need" and one "want" that you would like to make progress on in the year ahead?

How many hours a week do you spend on your personal goals? What do your efforts look like?

What do you love to do that you wish you did more often?

What are you an expert at? What did you do to become an expert?

Breathe. Be where you are. You've been broken down dozens of times and put yourself back together again. Think about how remarkable that is and how far you've come. You're not the same person you were a year ago, a month ago, or even yesterday. You're always growing . . . stronger!

Now that it's behind you, what did you do last week that was memorable?

If you could relive yesterday, what would you do differently?

What is the biggest change you have made in your life in the past year?

What do you understand today about your life that you did not understand a year ago?

What's the best decision you've ever made?

What do you do over and over again that you hate doing?

If you could choose one book as a mandatory read for all high school students, which book would you choose? Why?

Has your greatest fear ever come true? What is it, and how has it affected your life?

What is the most impactful thing you could do today in your personal life?

If happiness were the national currency, what kind of work would make you rich?

Go ahead and be a positive
force in the world today.
And remember, being positive
doesn't mean ignoring
the negative. Being positive means
overcoming the negative.
There's a big difference
between the two.

What word best describes the way you've spent the past month of your life?

What stands between you and happiness on an average day?

Is there ever a time when giving up makes sense?
When and how have you seen this play out in real life?

What is the meaning of "peace" to you? How do you
achieve this in your life? How often?

How do you find the strength to do what you know in your heart is right? Describe an example of a time when you did this successfully.

How short would your life have to be for you to start living differently today? What does "living differently" mean to you?

What's the difference between settling for things and accepting the way things are?

If today were the last day of your life, would you want to do what you are about to do today? Why?

What have you done in the past month that brings a sense of accomplishment?

What is your fondest memory from the past month?

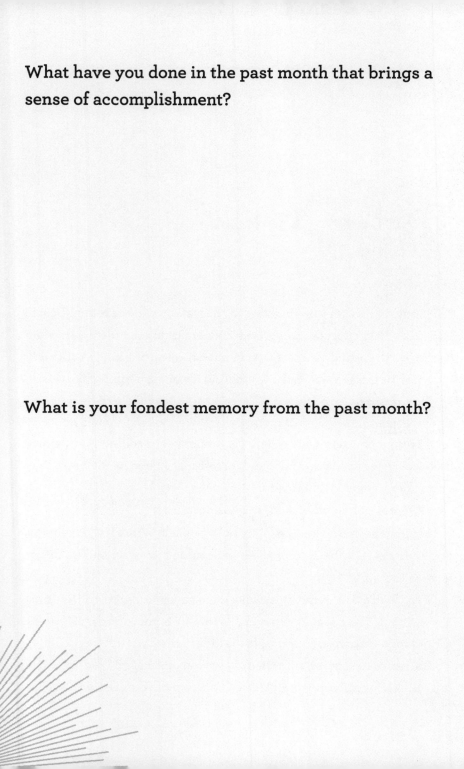

Together Is How

This morning, as we were relaxing at the water's edge of Miami Beach, I couldn't help eavesdropping on a conversation four teenagers were having on the beach blankets next to me. They were talking about making a positive difference in the world. And it went something like this...

"It's impossible to make a difference unless you're a huge corporation or someone with lots of money and power," one of them said.

"Yeah, man," another replied. "My mom keeps telling me to move mountains—to speak up and stand up for what I believe. But what I say or do doesn't even get noticed."

"Repression," another said, snickering.

I smiled because I knew exactly how they felt. When I was their age, I was certain I was being repressed and couldn't possibly make a difference in the world.

Eventually, one of the kids noticed me eavesdropping and smiling. He sat up, looked at me, and said, "What? Do you disagree?" As he waited for a response, the other three kids turned around too.

Rather than arguing with them, I stood up, took an old receipt out of my wallet, ripped it into four pieces, and wrote a different word on each piece. Then I crumpled the pieces into little paper balls and handed a different piece to each one of them. The kids were noticeably confused.

"Look at the word written on the paper I just handed you, and don't show it to anyone else." The kids followed my instructions and then glared back up at me. "You have two choices," I told them. "If your word inspired you to make a difference in this world, then hold on to it. If not, give it back to me so I can recycle the paper." They all returned their words without hesitation.

I sat down on the sand next to the kids' beach blankets and carefully laid out the four words they had just returned to me, so they could clearly see me combine the words one at a time to create a simple sentence: "I have a dream."

"Dude, that's Martin Luther King Jr.," one of the kids said.

"How did you know that?" I asked.

"Everyone knows Martin Luther King Jr.," the kid snarled. "We all had to memorize his speech in school last year."

"Why do you think your teachers had you memorize his speech?" I asked.

"I don't really care!" the kid replied. His three friends shook their heads in agreement. "What does this have to do with us and our situation?"

"Your teachers asked you to memorize those words, just like thousands of teachers around the world have asked students to memorize those words, because they have inspired millions of people, repressed or otherwise, to dream of a better world and take action to make their dreams come true. Do you see where I'm going with this?"

"Man, I know exactly what you're trying to do, and it's not going to work, all right?" said the fourth kid, who hadn't spoken a word until now. "We're not going to get all inspired and emotional over some historic speech. Our world is different now. And it's more screwed up than any of us can even begin to imagine, and there's little you or I can do about it. We're too small!"

I smiled again because I once believed and used to say similar things. Then, after holding the smile for a few seconds, I said, "On their own, 'I' and 'have' and 'a' and 'dream' are just words. Not very compelling or inspiring. But when you put them together in a certain order, they create a phrase that has been powerful enough to move millions of people to take positive action—action that changed laws, perceptions, and lives. You don't need to be inspired or emotional to agree with this, do you?"

The four kids just shrugged, but they struggled to appear totally indifferent, so I could tell they were listening. "And what's true for words is also true for people," I continued. "One person without help from anyone else can't do much to make a sizable difference in this crazy world—or to overcome all the various forms of repression that exist today. But when people get together and unite to form something more powerful and meaningful than themselves, the possibilities are endless."

Together is how mountains are moved. *Together* is how individuals create massive, life-changing results.

Who was the last person who was unexpectedly kind to you? What can you easily do to be a little kinder than usual today?

When was your first impression of someone totally wrong?

If you looked into the heart of someone who causes you stress and drama, what do you think you would find that is different from what is in your own heart?

If you could ask one person, alive or deceased, one question, who would you ask and what would the question be?

Is it more important to love or be loved? Why?

It's been said that grief is the price we pay for love. Do you agree? Who do you think of most now that they're gone?

Have you ever regretted something you did not say or do? What and when?

If today were the last day of your life, who would you call and visit, and what would you tell them?

What are you sure of in your life at this very moment?

What is the most valuable life lesson you learned from your parents or caregivers?

Just keep reminding yourself
that everyone you meet
is a human being who dreams
of something, fears something,
loves someone, and has
lost someone.
And . . . just keep being kind.

How would the world be different if you were never born? How is it different now because of your presence?

What makes you frustrated when you think about it? What eases this frustration in the long run?

What does love feel like, to receive and to give?

Who was the last person you said "I love you" to?
What do they mean to you?

What stresses you out more often than you would like to admit? Why?

What was the last thing that made you laugh out loud?

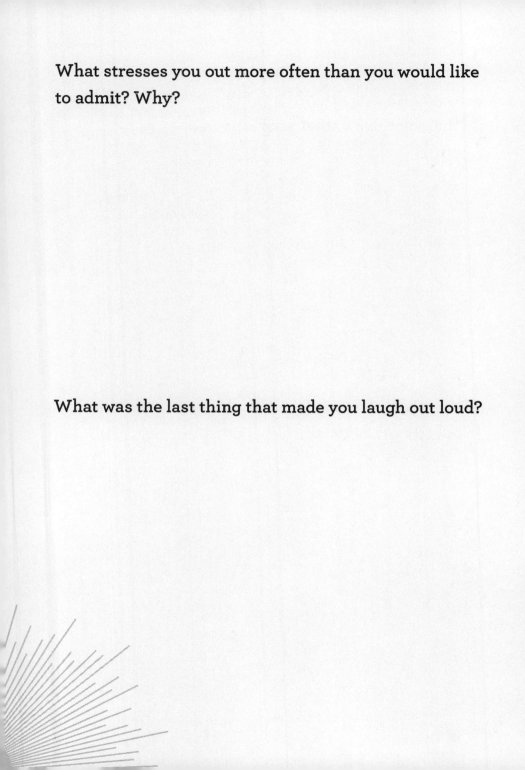

What is your biggest pet peeve about typical human behavior (things you often see others do, etc.)? Why do these actions bother you?

What are your favorite simple pleasures to notice in the world around you?

In what way have you made an effort to detach your emotions from the behavior of others?

What type of person inspires you the most?

Focus your energy today on cherishing those who lift you up, not on being sidetracked by those who don't. Remember, you may not be able to control the impolite things some people say and do to you, but you can decide not to be endlessly distracted by them.

When you meet someone for the first time, what do you want them to think about you?

How have you sabotaged yourself in the past five years? Who was there to help you sort things out?

If you had to move three thousand miles away, which three people and one thing would you miss the most? Why?

Who do you secretly envy? Why?

What is the greatest peer pressure you've ever felt?

What three questions do you wish you knew the answers to right now?

What's the biggest lie you once believed was true?

Who has been on your mind the most lately? Why?

What do you think is always worth waiting for?

Right off the top of your head, what is missing in your life today?

I Wish You Were Here

I would have preferred not to write to you. In fact, about a week ago, I put a Post-it Note on my computer monitor that said, "What would Skyman do?" (Skyman is my cat.) It was supposed to remind me not to do things that Skyman wouldn't do.

Skyman would just wag his tail or wiggle his little nose and hope that whoever he's wagging or wiggling at understands that he's hungry, or lonely, or in love, or whatever. But he certainly wouldn't write a silly love letter to the coolest girl he knows. Because he can't form complex thoughts. And because he's smart enough not to be so stupid.

This evening, the Post-it Note fell off my computer monitor and landed on the floor. And although Post-it Notes usually lose their stickiness after a few days, this one was different. It was still really sticky and shouldn't have come unstuck. And it was light green, which is the color of your eyes. These were obvious signs I couldn't ignore.

So I decided to write to you . . . to tell you that "Hanging by a Moment" is a totally awesome song. That Diet Coke tastes better when you smile. And that the world seems slightly easier to understand today than it did yesterday.

But still not as easy to understand as two days ago, when a friend and I shared a three-scoop 5 & Diner ice-cream sundae at midnight. And decided that some people are like hot fudge and others are like hard candy. And I don't remember why we decided that.

But it had something to do with friendship. And ice cream with two spoons instead of one. And later that night, after I dropped you off, I wanted to call you to ask whether you preferred hard candy or hot fudge, just to find out whether you'd sigh and giggle simultaneously when I asked. Because that's what I think you'd do.

I didn't call you, because Skyman wouldn't do that. He wouldn't even know how to dial your phone number. Because a cat's paws are not nearly as dexterous as human hands. Which must be nice for Skyman, because love is a lot simpler when you have paws.

Anyway, it's midnight again. And I'm sitting up in bed with my laptop thinking about how our lives begin and end in the time it takes the universe to blink. Which isn't too long. But long enough for letters that aren't too long. Letters that ramble instead of saying what they want to say. Which is . . .

I wish you were here. Just breathing beside me.

What is the primary quality you look for in a significant other?

What does it mean to allow another person to truly love you?

What's one good, recent example of someone with a negative attitude completely misjudging you? How did you handle it, and what did you learn?

What can you do to loosen the grip you have on yourself? How can you give yourself a little extra space and a little extra grace today?

What makes your significant other (or someone else you love) truly beautiful on the inside? What makes *you* truly beautiful on the inside?

When you think of home, what, specifically, do you think of?

For you personally, what and who are worth living for?

Who do you trust most and why?

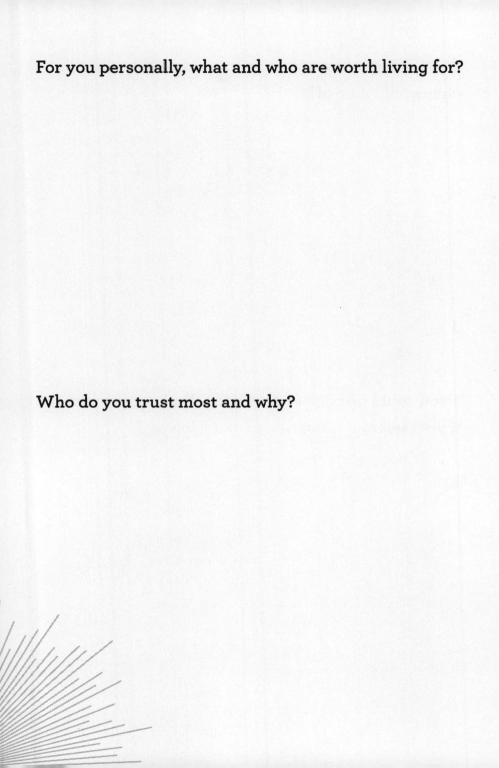

If you could take a single photo to represent your life, what would it be of?

If you could go back in time and tell a younger version of yourself one thing, what would you say?

If we have learned one thing from the past, it's that we need to be gentle with ourselves and others. We're all in this crazy world together, and we're all a bit weary and stressed. Be recklessly gracious today.

Excluding romantic relationships, who do you love and respect the most?

How will you embody love today? What does this mean to you?

In what ways are you your own worst enemy sometimes?

What chances do you wish you had taken in the recent past? In what ways is it *not* too late?

When is the reward worth the risk when it comes to love and trust?

What will you never do to yourself or others?

What book (or piece of writing) has had the greatest influence on your life and relationships? Why?

When you help someone, do you ever think, "What's in it for me?" In general, how does helping others help you help yourself?

What is the biggest challenge you face right now?
What progress have you made?

Would you rather have less work and more time or
have less time and more work you actually enjoy
doing? Why?

Prioritize your peace today. Some people will never understand, and it's not your job to teach or change them. Don't drive yourself crazy trying. Remember, learning to let go of certain expectations and to detach from certain people are two of the greatest paths to inner peace.

Would you rather be worried and well-informed or live in ignorant bliss? Why?

What three words would you use to describe your state of mind today?

Who and what do you think of when you think of trust?

How many people do you truly love and trust? Name the top two.

When you look at childhood photographs, what do you miss the most from that era of your life?

What is your happiest childhood memory?

What is your funniest childhood memory?

What has been the most rewarding aspect of growing older?

When was the last time you lost your temper? About what?

What is your biggest regret from the past year? How did you grow from this?

Think Better, Live Better

Reflect on these statements...

- I cannot control everything that happens; I can only control the way I respond to what happens. In my response is my power.

- I will never be as good as everyone tells me I am when I win, and I will never be as bad as I think I am when I lose.

- I will think less about managing my problems and more about managing my mindset. I will keep it positively focused.

- There is a big difference between empty fatigue and gratifying exhaustion. Life is short. As often as possible, I will invest in the activities that move me.

- If I don't have time for what matters, I will stop doing things that don't.

- My next step in the right direction does not have to be a big one.

- I will eat like I love myself, move like I love myself, speak like I love myself . . . and live like I love myself. Today.

- I will not get caught up in what could've been or should've been. I will look instead at the power and possibility of what is, right now.

- Peace will come to me when it comes from me.

- I will be too busy working on my own grass to notice if yours is greener.

The bottom line is, despite the real-world challenges you face, the biggest and most complex obstacle you will have to personally over-come on a daily basis is your own mind.

Yes, you can think better, which means you can tap into your inner strength and ultimately live better, one day at a time.

And yes, of course that's sometimes easier said than done.

Thinking better when you're in the heat of a tough season or at a crossroads in life takes guidance and practice. And that's why daily self-refection is so vital.

How has the discomfort you have felt in the past
helped you grow? How can you more gracefully
embrace the discomfort you presently feel?

What is the number one thing you want to accomplish
before you die? Why?

What did you learn recently that changed the way you live?

What do you imagine yourself doing ten years from now? How is it different from what you're doing today?

Do you own your things or do your things own you? In what way is your ego (or identity) attached to what you own?

What can money not buy? Name three specific things or outcomes in life.

What confuses you most about the meaning of life?

What new beginnings are transpiring in your life right now? What is changing before your eyes? Name at least three things.

What makes almost everyone smile?

Other than money, what have you gained from your current career or work?

Distancing yourself from someone who keeps giving you headaches and negative vibes is self-care. Stepping back from situations where you consistently feel unappreciated or disrespected is self-care. Today, choose to honor and respect your feelings and boundaries.

What healthy boundaries are not always enforced in your life and relationships?

What makes you feel uncomfortable? Why?

What hurts a little more than usual right now? How can you find some healthy relief?

When you look in the mirror, what do you see? What are the first few thoughts that come to mind?

What's one thing that has been occupying your attention lately that is *not* a high priority?

What little distractions get in the way of you being more present with the people you love?

What's one piece of life advice that you would give to your eighteen-year-old self?

What is one experience in your life where you exceeded what you believed was possible?

If you knew you could not fail, what would you start doing differently today?

When in the past did you do something even though you were scared? What did you do? How did it turn out?

Be where you are. That's where your power is. There's a time and place for everything, and every step is necessary. Just keep doing your best, and don't force what's not yet supposed to fit into your life. When it's meant to be, it will be.

What are two qualities you typically admire in others that you also possess right now?

What skill do you still want to learn? Why is it important?

Who is the first person you typically call with good news? Why do you want to share it with them first?

How do you feel about asking for help? When was the last time you asked? Who helped and how?

What's one little thing that you can do today to stretch your comfort zone (and that your future self might thank you for)?

What is something you have been putting off that brings you joy?

What two-minute task could you do now that will move you in the right direction today?

What are two healthy habits you've practiced consistently for over a year now?

What have you been resisting the most this week? How is this resistance affecting you?

Is there someone you wish would forgive you? Who and why?

AFTERWORD

"I have seen and touched and danced and sung and climbed and loved and meditated on a lifetime spent living honestly. Should it all end tonight, I can positively say there would be no regrets. I feel fortunate to have walked ninety years in my shoes. I am truly lucky. I really have lived 1,000 times over."

Those are the opening lines of the final entry in my grandmother Zelda's journal—a 270-page leather-bound journal she wrote small entries in almost every morning during the final decade of her life. In it, she reflected on lessons she had learned, lessons she was still learning, and the experiences that made these understandings possible.

When Zelda was diagnosed with terminal cancer on her ninetieth birthday, I sat with her in a hospital room for the entire day, in silence, in laughter, in tears, and in awe. Although her body was weak, her mind was intensely strong. The terminal diagnosis inspired her to think about her life and everything she had journaled about over the years, and reflect aloud. So I gave her the stage—my undivided attention—from sunrise until sunset.

As I sat beside her hospital bed, she thumbed through her journal one page at a time, reading dozens of specific entries she wanted me to hear. She spoke softly and passionately about her life, her loves, her losses, her pain, her dreams, her achievements, her happiness, and all the lessons that embodied these points of reference. It was without a doubt one of the most enlightening and unforgettable days of my life.

My grandmother passed away exactly two weeks later, peacefully in her sleep. The day after her passing, I found out she formally left her journal to me in her will. Since then, I have read it from cover to cover countless times.

Although I have shared many of her insights and quotes over the years with email subscribers, with coaching clients, and in our three traditionally published books, today, while I'm typing these words, would have been my grandmother's 105th birthday, so I'd like to end this journal by honoring her. To do so, I'm going to reshare excerpts of her journal entries that she shared with me in that hospital room fifteen years ago. I've done my best to sort, clean up, copyedit, and reorganize her wisdom into seven inspiring points. I hope you find value in them too.

1. **There are thousands of people who live their entire lives on the default settings, never realizing they can customize everything.** Don't settle for the default settings in life. Find your loves, your talents, and your passions, and embrace them. Don't hide behind other people's decisions. Don't let others tell you what you want. Design *your* journey every step of the way! The life you create from doing something that moves you is far better than the life you get from sitting around wishing you were doing it.

2. **The right journey is the ultimate destination.** The most profound and beneficial experience in life is not in actually achieving some-

thing you want but in seeking it. It's the journey toward an endless horizon that matters—goals and dreams that move forward with you as you chase them. It's all about meaningful pursuits—the "moving"—and what you learn along the way. Truly, the most important reason for moving from one place to another is to see what's in between. In between is where passions are realized, love is found, strength is gained, and priceless lifelong memories are made.

3. **Beginning each day with love, grace, and gratitude always feels better than the alternative.** When you arise in the morning, think of what an incredible privilege it is to be alive—to be, to see, to hear, to think, to love, to have something to look forward to. Happiness is a big part of these little parts of your life—and joy is simply the feeling of appreciating it all. Realize that it's not happiness that makes us grateful but gratefulness that makes us happy. Make a ritual of noticing the goodness that's already yours first thing in the morning, and you will see more goodness everywhere you look throughout the day.

4. **The willingness to do hard things opens great windows of opportunity.** One of the most important abilities you can develop in life is the willingness to accept and grow through times of difficulty and discomfort. Because the best things are often hard to come by, at least initially. And if you shy away from difficulty and discomfort, you'll miss out entirely. Mastering a new skill is hard. Building a business is hard. Writing a book is hard. Being married is hard. Parenting is hard. Staying healthy is hard. But all are amazing and worth every bit of effort you can muster. Realize this now. If you get good at doing hard things, you can do almost anything you put your mind to.

5. **Small, incremental changes end up transforming everything in the long run.** The concept of taking it one step at a time might seem absurdly obvious, but at some point we all get caught up in the moment and find ourselves yearning for instant gratification. We want what we want, and we want it now! And this yearning often tricks us into biting off more than we can chew. So remind yourself: you can't lift a thousand pounds all at once, yet you can easily lift one pound a thousand times. Tiny, repeated efforts will get you there, gradually.

6. **Almost no one wins a game of chess, or the game of life, by moving only forward.** Sometimes you have to move backward to put yourself in a position to win. Because sometimes, when it feels like you're running into one dead end after another, it's actually a sign that you're not on the right path. Maybe you were meant to hang a left back when you took a right, and that's perfectly fine. Life gradually teaches us that U-turns are allowed. So turn around when you must! There's a big difference between giving up and starting over in the right direction.

7. **New opportunities are always out there waiting for you.** Nobody gets through life without losing someone they love, something they need, or something they thought was meant to be. But it is these very losses that make us stronger and eventually move us toward future opportunities. Embrace these opportunities. Enter new relationships and new situations knowing that you are venturing into unfamiliar territory. Be ready to learn, be ready for a challenge, and be ready to experience something or meet someone that just might change your life forever.

And finally, as I'm wrapping up this short tribute to my grand-mother, I'm reminded of a poem by Christian D. Larson that she used to have hanging on her refrigerator when I was a kid. As soon as I was old enough to understand the poem, my grandmother made a photocopy of it for me, and more than thirty years later, I still have that same photo-copy laminated and hanging on my office bulletin board. These are words Angel and I do our best to live by every single day:

> Promise Yourself . . .
>
> To be so strong that nothing
> can disturb your peace of mind.
> To talk health, happiness, and prosperity
> to every person you meet.
>
> To make all your friends feel
> that there is something in them.
> To look at the sunny side of everything
> and make your optimism come true.
>
> To think only the best, to work only for the best,
> and to expect only the best.
> To be just as enthusiastic about the success of others
> as you are about your own.
>
> To forget the mistakes of the past
> and press on to the greater achievements of the future.
> To wear a cheerful countenance at all times
> and give every living creature you meet a smile.

To give so much time to the improvement of yourself
that you have no time to criticize others.
To be too large for worry, too noble for anger, too strong
    for fear,
and too happy to permit the presence of trouble.

To think well of yourself and to proclaim this fact to
    the world,
not in loud words but great deeds.
To live in faith that the whole world is on your side,
so long as you are true to the best that is in you.

ABOUT THE AUTHORS

Passionate writers, admirers of the human spirit, and full-time students of life, Marc and Angel Chernoff enjoy sharing inspirational advice and practical tips for life on their popular personal development blog, *Marc and Angel Hack Life*. Currently the site contains about six hundred articles on productivity, happiness, love, work, and general self-improvement, and has attracted seventy million page views since its inception in the summer of 2006. They are authors of the *New York Times* bestseller *Getting Back to Happy*, as well as *1000+ Little Things Happy, Successful People Do Differently* and *1000+ Little Habits of Happy, Successful Relationships*.

Marc and Angel both share a great passion for inspiring others to live to their fullest potential, and they honestly feel best when they are inspiring others to be their best. They started their blog with the goal of inspiring as many people as possible. And they work passionately every day to fulfill this goal through the thoughts and ideas they share online.

Please catch up with them at www.marcandangel.com.

Or you can email them:

angel@marcandangel.com and marc@marcandangel.com.

SUBSCRIBE FOR FREE

If you have enjoyed this journal and found it useful, you will love all the articles at *Marc and Angel Hack Life*. Readers continually leave feedback on how they have benefited tremendously from the site's material and how it's a staple for their personal growth.

By subscribing, you will receive free practical tips and inspirational advice geared for productive living, served fresh three times a week directly to your inbox.

LET'S CONNECT

We would love to hear from you and to know what you think. Feel free to get in touch with us via the following channels:

facebook.com/marcandangelhacklife

twitter.com/marcandangel

instagram.com/marcandangel

Also by Marc & Angel Chernoff

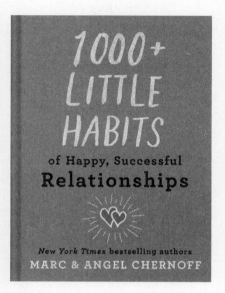

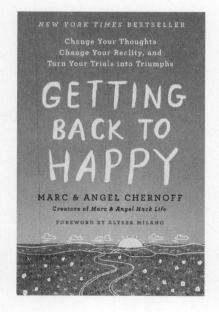